A CHINESE CRESTED DOG FOR ME

A CHINESE CRESTED DOG FOR ME . .because . . .

He is different.

He is unique.

He is exciting.

He has meticulous habits.

He comes in all colours from almost black to almost albino.

He can be pink in winter and a rich mahogany with flashy spots in summer.

He is a dog whose skin changes with the seasons.

He lacks doggy smell.

He washes himself like a cat.

He has a great sense of humour.

He talks.

He is an excellent house dog and guard.

He makes a super family pet, companion and friend.

He is an ideal size.

He loves you when you are down, celebrates with you when you are up.

He is a great conversation piece.

He enjoys a good walk and romp and equally enjoys your fireside, your home and your heart.

Cover illustrations are reproduced from original drawings by Sue Lovatt.

Best Wishes Mirrie Cardew

A Chinese Crested Dog for Me

MIRRIE CARDEW

CONTENTS

5 A Short History of the Breed
10 Choosing a Puppy
12 Feeding Your Puppy
12 Training Your Puppy
17 First Aid
18 Breeding
19 Caring for the In-Whelp Bitch
20 Whelping
26 Showing
30 Show Preparation
39 Some Do's and Don'ts
41 Questions and Answers
44 Brief History of the Xoloitzcuintli: First Dog of the Americas
44 Brief History of the Peruvian Inca Orchid Moonflower Dogs
45 Kennel Club Breed Standard of the Chinese Crested Dog
46 American Kennel Club Standard for Chinese Crested (Hairless)
47 American Kennel Club Standard for Chinese Crested (Powder Puff)
48 Useful Names and Addresses

ISBN 0 904597 64 4 Printed in England

Published by Midland Counties Publications
24 The Hollow, Earl Shilton, Leicester, LE9 7NA, UK.

A SHORT HISTORY OF THE BREED

Chinese Crested Dogs were in-being many hundreds and hundreds of years ago, possibly looking much as they do today. Doubtful if they originated in China, it is thought they migrated over the Bering Straights and had ancestors in Africa. Possibly rich Chinese merchants who settled in the South Americas and Mexico and Chinese sailors brought them in Clipper ships from the mainland and traded the little dogs for other commodities. In the Mexican Museum there is evidence of effigies of tiny hairless dogs being found in ancient Mexican tombs, long before the Aztecs arrived in the valleys. There are hairless dogs all over the world, and they go under many names: Chinese Crested Dogs, Mexican Xoloitzcuintil, African Hairless Dogs, Abyssinian and Sand Dogs, Turkish Naked Dogs, Peruvian Inca Moonflower Dogs etc etc. They all have two things in common —sparse teeth, often completely lacking pre-molars, and pricked or upright ears. Some are almost without any trace of hair but the great majority have a little tuft of hair on the skull and some between the toes and on the end of the tail.

They come in all colours and variations from near Albino to almost black. The sunlight affects the pigment under the skin and it is said that the Peruvian Inca Moonflower dogs were only allowed outside at night time to prevent their skin becoming a deeper colour, as it would in the sunlight.

There are many tales to be told — Christopher Columbus saw the hairless dogs with strange teeth, prick ears and a marked reluctance to bark. Darwin wrote that the hairless dogs had different teeth and it is thought to be some genetical quirk that links the hairlessness and dentition.

The little Chinese Crested Dog we know today is thought to have run true to type in South America for many years. From the late 1870s to 1904 they were exhibited in England, having been brought from Africa, China, Mexico and South America. Some had a crest of hair on the skull and most seemed to be elegant, graceful (having prick ears) and as active as cats. At the famous Crufts Dog show in 1928 folks flocked to see Mrs Lloyd's *Ting of Helouan*, an African Hairless Dog. The press had a great story talking about this tiny imported 'fever dog' that had no hair to protect him from the cold British winter. Mrs Forsyth (the former Mrs Lloyd) had bought him, and a hairless bitch *Minnie of Minea* in Egypt—where the natives, like the Mexicans, believed that if one touched a hairless dog it would cure an ill or fever.

Earlier, a London firm had acquired a pair of Abyssinian Sand Dogs with a cargo of reptiles. These dogs were of a sturdier type maybe more like the Mexican Hairless. When they were washed in hot soapy water they had flesh the colour of humans, rather pink. Both had prick ears and were very graceful and they too, behaved like cats.

The late Sydney Turner, and old friend of the late, famous and much endeared doggy expert A. Croxton Smith OBE, declared 'there was no distinctive breed in which hairlessness was an established character, although such dogs can be obtained in considerable number or proportion of descendants bred from hairless parents'.

right: Hairless Mexican Dog, Chesel theproperty of Mrs Fitzgerald.
below: African Hairless Dogs, Ting of Helouan and Minnie of Mineah, the property of Mrs Forsyth.
(photos by T. Fall)

Powder Puff St Erme Choc Ice at six months

The hairless dogs so often have siblings that are coated, obviously resembling some of their ancestry.

For many years in Britain the 'Powder Puffs' (as the coated dogs are now called) were rather frowned upon. It is true to say that unless one actually sees the puppy emerging from the dam, it is difficult to believe that one can be a typical fine-boned hairless puppy while the next, without any stretch of imagination, can grow into anything looking like a miniature Shih Tzu to a larger Tibetan Terrier — various textures of coat, ranging from sparse harsh or soft coat, to long and silky or long and fluffy. I have seen 'Powder Puffs' with almost smooth coats to a mixture of wire hair. Most of these puppies in the nests look cuddlesome, attractive and fluffy — but they are no doubt survivors, being as tough as old boots and so tenacious.

Most 'Powder Puffs' unlike their hairless siblings have good dentition, whereas the hairless dogs mostly have far fewer molars and as often as not the pre-molars are conspicuous by their absence. The canine teeth often protrude forward; rather 'pre-historic looking' to say the least.

Today, however the Chinese Crested Dogs seem to have come to stay as a popular pet and show dog. Thanks to a dedicated bunch of enthusiasts here and in the 'States there are some lovely specimens in the show ring. I think one should mention Mrs Ruth

Staround Inca drawn by Dierdre Ashdown.

Harris who was responsible for most of our lovely dogs today, going back to her famous *Staround* line. She must have spent a great deal of time and money importing from a famous line in the USA, which was later complemented by stock from the famous Gypsy Rose Lee. Many lovely 'Cresteds' have won top honours in the show ring here, well before the required number of registrations qualified them for Championship status.

I had the pleasure of giving the beautiful *Staround Inca* (owned by Mrs Crowther Davies) her first of many First Prizes at an all-breed show, at Wigston in Leicestershire over fifteen years ago. *Inca* won 'Best of Breed' at the big London Brent show in 1971, when Chinese Cresteds had classes scheduled for them for the first time in history.

The Chinese Crested Dog Club was founded in 1969 and had its first breed show on 24 September 1974. Thanks to the dedicated breeders and enthusiasts, it has gone from strength to strength. It is the official club of the breed in the United Kingdom. Although with bands of enthusiasts growing all the time, no doubt we shall have more clubs eventually as have other breeds. The American Chinese Crested Club was organised in 1975 followed by the first-ever match for the breed.

The Chinese Crested dog is remarkably healthy and hardy. His temperature is slightly higher than his coated brothers, and although he does not care for the wind and rain, he seems to delight in the snow. He makes an ideal pet and companion, is an excellent house dog and (would you believe it) guard. He will give early warning of anyone approaching your home day or night. He is a smart little chap and often reminding one of a prancing pony, with his tossing crest and furnishings on his feet and tail. Our original crested dog born in 1972 actually went out with the gun, accompanying my son with a mixed gun dog family of Chihuahua, Basenji, Crested and Fox Terrier. The crested is very adaptable and fits into any mood and situation.

CHOOSING A PUPPY

Until recent years it was usual for one to have ones name on a list to acquire one of these exotic dogs. Now they are more numerous, and with luck one can contact owners and exhibitors at shows who just may have a puppy to spare. I honestly think they are far too an intelligent breed to be shut away in kennels for long periods. They are exceptionally clever and I'm sure most breeders give much personal attention and care to their litters.

I would recommend a would-be owner to seek out the 'Crested' benches at a show and chat-up the owners who are always ready to talk about their beloved pets. Whether you choose a dog or a bitch is up to you - it is a well known fact that owners like to keep the bitch puppies, hoping to increase and improve their dogs. Usually, the price of a good bitch is fairly high, especially when you think how much original stock costs. A new puppy is a new responsibility and a new friend; taking a puppy into the family is like having another child - a full time job. I think I would like to see the parents of the puppy if possible. A nervous dog of any breed is a constant worry. On the whole, Chinese Cresteds are terrific extroverts and from the tender age of six weeks look like a miniature adult — super if you can choose one with a glamourous crest and lovely tail and feet fringes. On the other hand look closely. Has the puppy hair in other places, like up his spine or extending up his legs and tail? I think you will find the softer supple skin on a puppy who may be not so well furnished. I personally love dogs as pets; they are perhaps a little more independent and often seem to have a little more character. Bitches, like female humans, are more complex and who says they are the weaker sex! A new puppy's happiness and future is in your hands now.

Chinese Crested puppy at seven weeks St Erme Wild Orchid (Australian Champion) photo by Tony Cardew

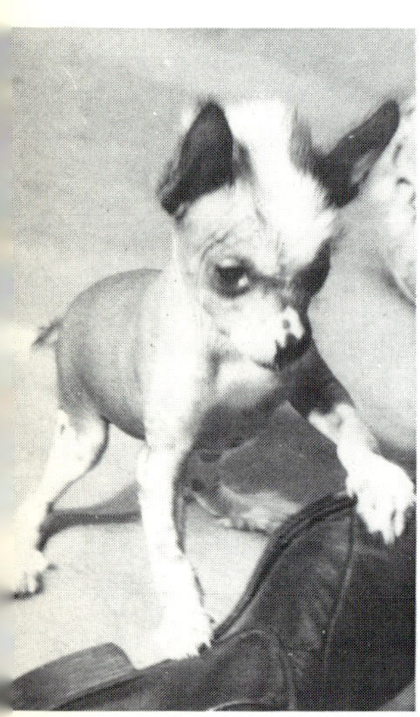

Vaccinations are most sophisticated these days, and give maximum immunity against such infections as distemper, hardpad, hepititus, canicola, leptospirosis and the dreaded parvo virus. A vet is your, and your dogs best friend — prevention is better than cure and usually far cheaper.

It is usual for a puppy to go to his new home at twelve weeks. By this time he ought to have been properly weaned, wormed and vaccinated, and be safe to take out even if he has to have a later booster. A reliable breeder will supply you with a diet sheet, his pedigree, and Kennel Club Registration Certificate. It is usual for expensive puppies to be given full insurance cover for at least six weeks. This is a sensible idea as it covers both parties. Avoid, if at all possible, any sort of breeding terms, you want the puppy to be yours with no ties, which rarely seem to work out to be equally fair to both parties.

Dutch & Int. Champion St Erme Dancing Moppet and pup.

FEEDING YOUR PUPPY

When you take him home, he ought to be eating three meals a day. At 8am, my twelve-week old puppies have a cup of warm milk with added vitamins, and cereal (Weetabix, cornflakes, porridge or baby cereal) to which is added a scrambled egg, plus a few rusks or puppy biscuits to chew. At noon, fresh minced meat and scalded puppy meal mixed with a little grated carrot or green vegetable if available. At 4pm, maybe a little boiled rice with a little flaked fish or chicken plus a drink of milk. There are many products on the market, but keep your puppy to the diet he is used to and only change gradually. You can get him used to different tastes; fish, rabbit and chicken are most appetising and nutritious, but do take care never to feed bones from these. All our puppies and adults have safe knuckle bones to chew, far better a puppy does his chewing on a bone than on your best shoes. Chewing keeps him happy and occupied, is good for his teeth and gums and is a rich source of nourishment into the bargain. You will find your pet shop and supermarket a treasure house of pet foods and accessories. Nine and a half million households have pets in Britain, so pet food is big business and much thought and research is put into it. Most of the recognised brands of food will be alright for your dog. If however you are lucky and have a good butcher who can sell you fresh meat and offal (such as tripe and hearts) and safe marrow bones, your Chinese Crested will indeed be in clover. An adult Chinese Crested needs one very good nourishing meal a day plus a snack. Cresteds tend to be greedy dogs and often give one the impression this might be their last meal.

TRAINING YOUR PUPPY

One assumes your puppy has been fully vaccinated so you can take him out of doors. So now get him used

Ch Heathermount Pharoah of Moonswift. Owner Diana Bowter-Townsend. (photo: F. Garwood)

to a soft collar, a cat collar is ideal at first or a soft leather one. The harder man-made plastic collars often chafe a young puppies neck. Cresteds do not really like wearing collars, so the sooner he gets used to one the better. If you have a garden, take him outside as soon as he has had his meal. You will have the odd accident but on the whole Cresteds are creatures of habit and once shown what is expected of him soon understand. If you have a flat, I know many toy dogs can be trained to a cat litter tray. Yet it is far better to give him the freedom of a garden where he can run and find the ideal spot to make a pool and mess which he will always return to. A cardboard box with a small (not wool) blanket or towel makes a perfect bed, especially if it can be put in a warm corner of the kitchen, with perhaps a sheet of newspaper on the floor, in case of the odd accident the first few nights. A bone will keep him happy and amused, as he is sure to miss mother and litter mates at first.

If you allow him into your bed, he will expect to be there every night. Remember dogs are creatures of habit, once allowed always allowed, once forbidden always forbidden. It is not fair to allow him on the best chairs one day and smack him the next. So give him his own corner from the start, and make an extra fuss of him when he is good.

When you introduce him to a lead he ought to have got used to his collar. One of the best ways to train a puppy to walk on a lead is to take him to a quiet spot,

Alltot Royal Heiress - first ever Powder Puff to be Best of Breed in this country. Owned by S.G. & J.A. Gorwill. Photo: Lionel Young.

St Erme Swanky Doodle (Frosty) at 12 weeks from a drawing by Sue Lovatt.

chat him up gently and encourage him to follow you. An important don't, do not yank the lead as this can put him off walks for some time. I find Cresteds are quick to learn and if you make the lesson short and enjoyable for both of you, moving off at a brisk pace, speaking encouraging words, perhaps offering a tasty titbit as he gets the message. Often an older dog will help as the puppy will try to follow suit. Another way is to follow the puppy around in the direction he is going until he gets used to the lead. Above all patience is a great virtue. If you are both exasperated, give the lesson up and try another day. Most puppies are happier just playing loose in the garden. I have to admit some of my most successful show winners in hound, terrier and toy breeds went on a lead for the first time only a day or so before their first show.

Training proper can begin at around four or five months. If you live in a town the local canine society can put you in touch with the various training and ringcraft classes. These can be fun and beneficial to both dog and owner. If your dog is taught to sit and heel they are useful lessons to know, if he is going to have the pleasure of running free in the park and you want him back quickly. I have to admit (The Hairless) Cresteds are not the most obedient breed and like a few other toy and Tibetan and hound breeds have a mind of their own. I think they have exceptionally good noses and often a keen scent gets the better of them. On trips to the park one meets other owners, exchanges experiences, your pet gets used to other dogs and that too is an advantage if you take him to a show.

Although most pet owners just want a companion, remember you are going to feed and care for your dog for possibly ten years or more. So it is to your advantage to have a smart sweet natured pet in blooming health, never take a runt or a puppy with a defect, it will be a constant worry even if you do feel sorry for it. Thank goodness most breeders wish to keep a good

Sandcrest Blue Print, owned by Mrs G. G. Mallinson.

reputation and will take an interest in the puppies future, and maybe encourage you to show it. An adult Crested living in town will be happy with two walks a day, he can then be left to play around the house and garden. If the weather is fine Cresteds love to be outdoors, just make sure he has a draught proof box to get into if he wishes. A much loved dog is usually in good show condition. If he is stroked and patted and has a scrupulously clean bed to sleep in he will seldom need bathing. Yet Cresteds love baths and providing you use a baby shampoo or a non-perfumed one and dry him carefully, rubbing a little baby oil into his skin afterwards, especially if he has been out in the sun and it has become a trifle dry. I think these clever dogs need much love and companionship and are so much easier to live with if pampered somewhat.

FIRST AID

Emma with Alltot May-Lou (two reserve CCs). Perry's daughter by the late Mei-Lee of Peking. Owner Mrs S. Gorwill. Photo: Lionel Young.

Apart from infections (which are now mostly covered with excellent vaccines and antibiotics) and barring accidents your pet ought to be set for a long healthy life. If he does get involved in an accident make sure he is kept as quiet as possible. It is useful to have a sedative from your vet in your first aid box, and an aerosol for stings and scratches. Eye lotion will aid removing specs of dust from the eye. If he should be bitten by another dog it is advisable to get him to the vet as quickly as possible. A penicillin injection can prevent a nasty abscess and complications later on. A torn ear can be held together between two sterile wipes until the bleeding stops. A few grains of permanganate of potash will often stop bleeding if pressed to the wound on a sterile pad. A puppy that may have taken poison may be tempted to take a little milk before you get him and a sample of the poison to the vet as quickly as possible. Keep your vets telephone number handy at all times; better to be prepared and hope nothing serious ever happens, at least you cannot reproach yourself if you take all sensible precautions.

Most Cresteds come into season every seven months or so. In fact I had a Powder Puff who came into season every six months to the day. Her two Hairless sisters who shared the fireside with two Basenjis — I find Cresteds and Basenjis identical in habit and character — came in season only once a year like the Basenjis. There are several symptoms of season or 'heat' — ususally the bitch is even more fussy and affectionate, her vulva begins to swell and she has a red discharge that tends to change to orange around the 11th to 13th day when she is at her most fertile. Occasionally, a bitch who is so clean in her ways, may have been in season for a few days before it becomes noticeable. This is often why some folk think a bitch needs mating far earlier than she does. I'm all for leaving a bitch until she has fully matured before mating — puppyhood is so short after all. For bitches I do not wish to breed from, a hormone shot from the vet is most effective and much easier if one wants to keep the boys and girls together. It is a good idea to consult your vet before the season begins, although I find getting the hormone into the bitch within the first forty-eight hours of her season usually stops it until her next cycle. For many years I had bitches on the pill with no side effects whatsoever. One bitch went on to have a litter of six, having had her seasons suppressed for three years.

You will naturally have thought about a suitable stud dog. If you have gone to shows you will have possibly seen his offspring. If you can manage to take your bitch to a top show dog as well as heritage then you ought. A beautiful animal however near perfection is no earthly good unless he has a lovely outgoing temperament to go with his looks. A top show winner has usually got that little extra personality that has got him there in the first place.

It is usual to take the bitch to the dog around the 12th day of her season. If you take her too early the dog may be keen but the bitch will just 'Go' for him as he advances upon her. She could be extremely rude and aggressive towards him and possibly try to bite him, in which case you will not be very popular with the dogs owner — it will be very frustrating and unsettling and a great deal of time will have been wasted. With reasonable luck the bitch will mate around the 11th to 13th day. They will probably 'tie' for about twenty minutes, then you can take her home. The late Countess Howe, who I knew as a youngster, had famous Labradors as well as Pugs and always maintained never to mate a bitch more than once. I have found this sensible advice over the years. I know some people will mate a bitch several times, so keen are they for puppies. Although unlikely, it can result in puppies of different age if the bitch did take to a multiple mating, often causing a premature litter into the bargain. There is usually a choice of about four or five days (from the 9th to the 14th) when the bitch will stand to the dog. I find my most successful litters have come from the later days of her season.

CARING FOR THE IN-WHELP BITCH

You will discover once the Chinese Crested has been successfully mated, her season will soon be over. However, do not let her loose with other dogs for another two weeks, just to be on the safe side.

Now is the time to check and see if she is due for any booster vaccinations — better to ensure as full immunity as possible for her unborn offspring. Your vet may suggest worming her again although it is usual practice to worm your dog regularly for both round and tape worm. It is possible to buy preparations from your pet shop, but it is often cheaper and more satisfactory to acquire any drugs and medications from your vet. There are available some excellent tablets for toy dogs that are gentle and safe as well as most effective, so ask your vet.

Let your bitch lead as normal life as possible for

the first four to five weeks. Then you should see a definite thickening around her middle, especially after her food. You can give her extra protein in the way of meat, fish and eggs but do not feed her late at night unless you want her to get you up. You could divide her meals into three smaller ones so as not to overload her tummy. Let her have her usual exercise and see she has plenty of fresh air. After the 5th week let her take life at her pace and make sure her food is nourishing for the sake of the dam as well as her ensuing family. I find Cresteds tend to be very active until the final few days and have decided their puppies must be good sailors. See that she has her usual vitamin tablets, but as my vet recommends, do not over do the calcium tablets.

It is a good idea to organise her whelping quarters in good time. If she is a house pet it is easy to give her a nice box, preferably with sides and a roof. I have a low voltage pet heater which I put in the box underneath the very superior Vetbed that you can buy at any doggy store. My nautical son tells me these were first originated to keep the deep sea divers warm and dry; they are now used extensively in hospitals and for new born babies. These substantial doggy blankets are perfect to accept new puppies as they absorb any wet and the puppy feels snug from birth. The dams seem less keen to scratch them up into a heap as they do a blanket. You can also give her a sheet of paper if she is the paper tearing kind. Anyhow it is a good idea to get her sleeping in this box during the last two weeks.

WHELPING

The normal time for a bitch to carry her puppies is sixty-three days, nine weeks after she was mated. Most bitches go the full term, but occasionally one carrying a large litter may decide to whelp up to three days earlier, although I have had a bitch who went five days late. She was under veterinary supervision and showed no signs of whelping until one hour before she produced two very small but healthy puppies, who incidentally opened their eyes at exactly six days old.

In most breeds it is noticeable to see a colourless discharge from the vulva a few days before whelping. I find this more usual in a coated Powder Puff than the Hairless bitch, who is most fastidious in her personal hygiene. A sure sign of her due to whelp is a drop in her temperature, so a blunt headed thermometer is useful, although I think one can now get the latest skin measuring thermometer. You will find her looking a trifle shivery so do keep an eye on her and watch her movements — is she making a nest or seeking a dark corner? If you are in the slightest fussed about her, ring your vet. Cresteds are quite easy whelpers in fact the easiest of all the toy breeds we have had over the past forty year. She may pant and scratch before actually straining (in labour proper). Cresteds too tend to have quite a good meal unlike many breeds who go off food just before whelping, as if preparing for a good lie in.

Once she really begins to scratch and pant you may find that she wants you at her side for a little moral support. Like Basenjis, I find Cresteds some time make a devil of a fuss just before the first puppy, then settle down and take it all in their stride with no problems. After many years of being organised with a blanket for the puppies, loads of towels scissors and what have you, my vet has at last made me leave the bitches entirely alone. Just talking to them and being there helps. Many owners love to poke, push and look, more often than not upsetting the little mother into the bargain. Cresteds are clever little dogs and know exactly what to do, even young maiden bitches, so just wait and observe. After a few pushes she may want to rest for a while and when her pains begin again she will possibly give one or two little grunts and the first water sac will appear.

This is not the puppy but a membrane sac of greenish coloured liquid which eases the passage of the puppy and acts like a cushion gently dialating the vaginal passage. When the bag bursts the puppy is not usually far behind. It is normal for the puppy to come head first but Cresteds seem to stretch very easily and the puppy often emerges with a 'plop' before you know where you are. Do not interfere or pull on the cord as this, attached to the placenta, usually takes a little longer to be pushed out. The mother will vigorously lick her whelp and sever the cord with her teeth. If she has difficulty you can gently break the cord with your fingernails, but not before the placenta (afterbirth) has arrived. You may cause trouble if you try to snip the cord and let the afterbirth go back into the bitch. If you feel she is being slow at this point you can just clear the membrane from the puppies face, but do not worry if the puppies stay in their sacs for what seems ages, they are quite OK. Leave everything to your clever little bitch, more harm is done to toy puppies by over anxious owners so my vet says. It is important that the bitch eats the afterbirth; I used to take them away and count them and think they upset the bitch, but no, they contain all the nutrients and help more than anything to establish her milk bar.

Heat is most important to new born puppies, almost more than nourishment for the first forty-eight hours, so ensure they have a nice warm bed. The puppy will dry quickly, far better that the mother licks it and forms a bond than you try to take it away and fuss about towelling it etc, however sterile you think everything is. You will know at once if you have a Hairless or a Powder Puff, as you can usually see the crest and small amount of hair on the tail. Hairless puppies born pink usually develop pigment as the days and weeks go by and an all white puppy may well turn out to be a glamorous spotted one. The Powder Puff may look quite dark at birth but turns a gorgeous golden or silver colour. You will find the whelp will try to suck at once, often whilst the rest of his cord and placenta has still to emerge — this is wonderful as he gets the valuable antibodies from the mother's milk, so vital for his survival. It is amazing how tenacious Cresteds are, especially the Powder Puffs with puppies arriving at intervals from a few minutes up to an hour or so. Sometimes a bitch will have a good rest in the middle of whelping, then as her pains start up again she will start pushing and soon the last of her brood will be here. When you think she has finished you can offer her a drink of milk laced with glucose and maybe she will even take a little minced beef or chicken. Mostly though she will want to rest, so try and get her to make a pool in the garden and if you can replace her Vetbed with a dry clean one all the better. The Cresteds do not get very messy hindquarters as do other breeds and a quick wipe around with a sterile wipe will make her comfy. If you have a Powder Puff whelping a good idea is to clip her quarters and tummy to keep her as clean and comfy as possible, her coat will soon recover. Once the bitch has settled, leave her alone, the puppies will mew as they try to find their way around the box but they are far able to settle quickly if left strictly alone. If by any chance the bitch has not settled, the chances are she may have another puppy or maybe an afterbirth has got left behind. If so, do not hesitate to consult your vet, who should have been put in the picture in any case.

I assure you Chinese Cresteds are one of the easiest whelpers and more than likely you will just find her with a beautiful nest of babies, although it is better to be all ready and be sure of a warm place to call her own. One can buy expensive whelping boxes with roll bars around to prevent the babies being sat on, but I find even a maiden bitch will be happy in a roomy box providing that it is warm and dry with a good Vetbed or similar heavy duty washable mat being ideal.

If the litter is full term it is a good idea to get your vet to remove their dew claws at three to four days. If premature leave until the fifth day. This is a quick operation and prevents caught and damaged dew claws that can be such a nuisance as well as unsightly in an adult dog. Also check the back feet as many Hairless carry double dew claws often on all four feet.

Many Chinese Crested owners say their bitches do not have all that milk. I have had only one problem bitch. We did find hand rearing the Powder Puff gave her three Hairless puppies more of a chance, where on the other hand, a sturdy Powder Puff sucking lustily can stimulate the milk galnds far better than a weakling puppy. So the idea seems to be leave all the babies with their mother and see she has maximum nourishment and maybe supplement the stronger Powder Puffs from three weeks, maybe weaning them a little earlier than their Hairless siblings. I always let the babies stay as long as they wish with the dam, providing she can escape from them if they get a bit much — possibly into a nearby chair or box. You will find your bitch will want to stay most of the time with her babies, possibly up to three or four weeks. If the litter are fat and content, leave them until they are about three-and-a-half to four weeks and introduce a little baby cereal and milk to their box. Mother will lap and in no time at all the babies will be in the dish. I introduce scraped (yes - a bit expensive) meat from three weeks just as much as will sit on your thumb nail. In no time they will snatch it from your fingers. The mother will need two nourishing meals a day plus two milky snacks.

From six weeks our puppies had the following: at 8am baby cereal or Weetabix with warm full cream cows milk (goats milk is marvellous as is Welpi a proprietry brand) to which I add one egg yolk for every two puppies and a crushed vitamin tablet. At noon, the first size puppy meal (scalded with hot water or gravy) plus ½oz per puppy of fresh raw mince or Pedigree Puppy food (which contains all the nutrients your puppy needs) plus a drink of milk. At 4pm scrambled egg or rice pudding plus a drink and at 8pm a little finely minced chicken or fish with a little baby cereal gives a substantial meal to last the puppy through the night. Mother is usually with them at night until eight weeks. Cut down to two meals and a snack at three months and two meals at six months.

By the time the puppies are six weeks you may wish

Above: Mrs Foster Parker's Heathermount Xotic.

Right: the author's St Erme Exotica at seven months drawn by Sue Lovatt

to advertise them in the dog journals or local papers. Make sure they are properly weaned and wormed before they go to new homes, our puppies are gentle wormed at five, seven and nine weeks of age. Puppies can now be vaccinated at four weekly intervals from six weeks, your vet will be able to advise you.

Get the puppies registered in good time and its so much nicer if you can hand over the puppy complete with all his papers and so save being bothered with them later. Make sure he is going to the kind of home where he will be treasured and have some quality of life and where he will be regarded as number one. Its also nice if he can be shown and to be shown will be a credit to you. Also, owning a good dog is a great pleasure, always something nice to look upon, even if he never gets to Crufts. It is an excellent idea to take out puppy insurance to safeguard all interests.

SHOWING

To show your Chinese Crested, he must be registered at the Kennel Club and his registration certificate should be duly signed by the breeder and handed to you complete with a signed pedigree certificate when you purchase the puppy. Most breeders are helpful to novices and only too thrilled if you show their puppy. After all, if he is a nice one, it is a good advertisement for them and means they still keep in touch with their stock. In Great Britain there are numerous shows from small members Sanction shows to the major championship shows such as the famous Crufts.

There are two weekly dog journals of high repute which have been going for years and cover every aspect of dogdom, these being *Our Dogs* and *Dog World*. There are several other doggy magazines that can be found at your news stand . The journals are weekly papers and give all the details of where the shows are, classes and judges, show reports, as well as breeding notes about your particular breed — in fact a mine of information to any 'doggy' enthusiast and a bible to most of us. I took *Our Dogs* (it cost just 4d — four old pence) when I was at school and it gave me many hours of enjoyment as a youngster during the war. I just dreamt of all the lovely dogs I wanted and actually did have eventually; not such a bad dream for youngsters these days.

Dog Shows fall roughly into four categories:

a) Exemption Shows
b) Sanction Shows and
Limited Unbenched Shows.
c) Open Shows
d) Championship Shows

Exemption Shows are mostly 'Fun Shows' and often organised to benefit a charity and are exempt from Kennel Club Rules. They are usually advertised in the local paper and you can enter on the day.

Sanction Shows and Limited Unbenched Shows are usual local events, often organised for the benefit of

Champion Clogheen Donna. Owner Mrs Mary Smith. (photo by U.K. & E.A. McFarlane)

members of local dog clubs. They are a good 'stepping-stone' for your puppy to higher shows. Champions cannot be shown.

Open Shows are open to all comers, including champions and are often organised in conjunction with the many big agricultural shows up and down the country during the summer. These are usually 'benched' and often have classes for the Chinese Crested. They can be an interesting day out for all the family and ideal for taking out your puppy and meeting fellow enthusiasts.

Championship Shows (of which 'Crufts' is the most famous) are those where most of the breeds are catered for and the majority of the breeds can compete for the much highly-prized Kennel Club Challenge Certificate, commonly known among the dog folk as C. Cs. One is offered to the best of sex in a breed. To add the coveted 'Champion' in front of a dogs name, the dog has to win three Challenge Certificates, under three different judges. There can be over fifty Cresteds now at a big show, so C.C.s are not easy to come by. The championship shows are always benched — your dog has to be put in a wire cage on a bench and remain there most of the show time. This enables interested fee-paying spectators to look upon him. It can be a very long and tiring day for both dog and exhibitor, especially if much travelling is involved (to say nothing of the expense, as entry fees go up all the time).

After a show, it is usual for the judge to write a report, on prize winners. These are published in the 'doggy' press, from which one can glean the faults or virtues of a dog.

If I were to take a Chinese Crested to a show, possibly a small local show to begin with, I would ensure that my puppy was fully vaccinated and as fit and healthy as possible. I would then find a small show in my area, and enter the puppy in suitable classes i.e. Minor Puppy Dog (for puppies six to nine months); Puppy Dog (a puppy up to twelve months); Maiden Dog (for a puppy or dog that has never won a first prize) and possibly an 'Any variety toy puppy or novice' class. The entry fee and membership to this kind of show is usually around £1.00.

I would take along a few tit-bits to bribe him to follow me the few paces I am expected to walk in the ring (such as a little cooked chopped liver, chicken or heart). I would also take along my 'doggy bag' containing a damp face cloth, a little baby powder and baby cream — this works wonders if your puppy was sick in the car and you can rub him over and powder his crest and tail. You want him to go into the ring looking bandbox fresh so make sure you brush it all out before entering the ring.

Your class will be called, and this you will know from the catalogue you bought at the door and from your original entry from the schedule. You will be allocated a number in the ring, so take along a safety pin or maybe your swish club badge to attach this number to your suit or dress.

If your puppy walks well on his collar leave it at

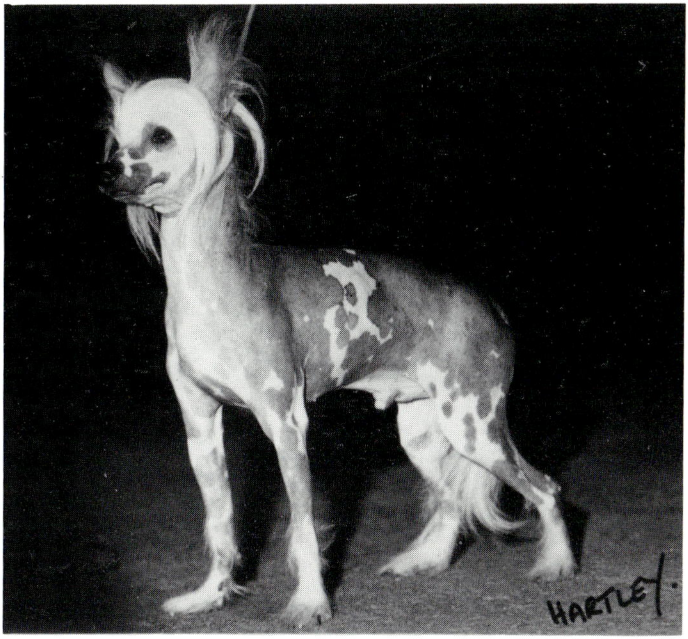

Ch Clogheen Perry owned by S.G. & J.A. Gorwill.

that. You can buy smart show collars but the most important factor is that your puppy is used to it.

You will stand in a line with all the other exhibitors, then the steward will ask you to put your puppy on the table to enable the judge to examine him at close quarters. He will look at his teeth and feel his body, then ask you to put him on the floor and walk him. Some judges like you to make a triangle, this way the judge can see the dog from all angles. The judge will assess his type and confirmation according to the standard of each individual breed. When the judge makes his final assessment you will be expected to stand as quietly as possible and have your dog looking up at you and wagging his tail if at all possible, then you may be in with a good chance. Chinese Cresteds love to show off and this is the clue to a born show dog.

If you are lucky and come away with a prize it will have made your day, but remember there is an old saying 'Every Champion has at least five faults and the perfect dog has yet to be born'. Also, humans being what they are, each has a different eye and one dog that pleases another may not please another.

Once bitten by the show bug life can be an endless source of entertainment. You make many friends, and need never be lonely. The dogs have no class distinction; one is on equal terms with everyone else.

If you have a real star of a dog — that means not only one that fits the standard, but one that has that 'personality plus' — then indeed you will enjoy your Chinese Crested all his days whether he is shown or not.

SHOW PREPARATION

THE CHINESE CRESTED HAIRLESS

Your hairless puppy ought to fit the standard as much as possible, remembering that no dog is perfect. If he is going to be shown, make sure he is in as good body condition as possible, but this is not always easy with dogs who are keen on bitches or maybe a trifle love-lorn. Grilled breast of lamb is a great conditioner; good for the skin and puts on weight fast. Pull the meat from the bones — we give the bones to the cats who adore them — and serve warm, mixing the juices with some boiled rice or a little puppy meal. Even 'faddy' feeders seldom refuse this.

left: Staround Quanto
right: Clogheen Martello

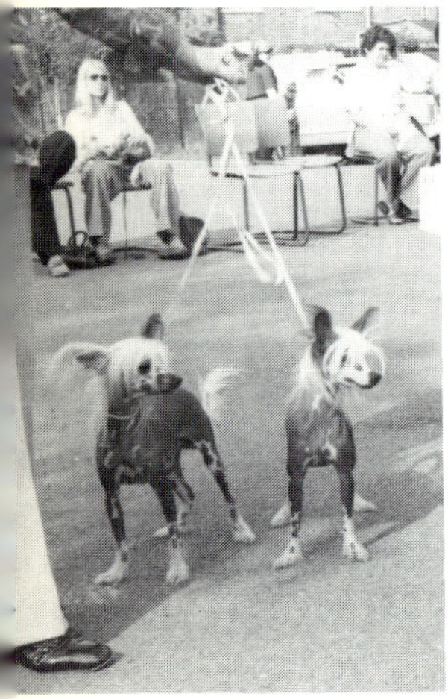

A good hot bath two days before the show helps to shed dead skin and open pores where dust may have collected. Bath with a good unperfumed or baby shampoo, as some of the medicated shampoos are a little strong for toy breeds, especially the hairless dogs, who will lick the shampoo as you put it on. Take good care to pat dry in a large warmed towel; fortunately they do dry quickly, and a little baby powder between the toes and on the crest helps to make him feel comfy. Pay attention to the ears, as so many Cresteds seem to get encrusted skin around the ear edges, and a weekly rub with vaseline will cure this. After his bath, rub a little baby oil into his body; any chafed places will respond quickly to a little medicated baby cream applied overnight.

If his skin has become very dirty playing around the garden or living in not so scrupulous quarters, rub plenty of vaseline into him and cover with a home made cotton or towelling coat, made from an old tea towel folded and stitched — ideal and washable! Following this, leave overnight or for a few hours then give him a nice warm bath as above.

Some people tend to over-trim Cresteds, which is not really necessary. A judge will forgive a few stray hairs on the face, and shaving and hair removing cream can usually be detected by the judge, apart from leaving the little dog sore.

Hellesveor China Doll of Tonor (Suki). Bred by Barbara Mills, owned and adored by Norma & Tony Hill. Photo by G. Foyle.

Some hairless youngsters seem to have a few blackheads, and this is usually more noticeable on the paler colours. Thorough cleanliness is the answer — do not pluck or squeeze as this can result in nasty and infectious spots. Your vet can give you a cream to help, also, good diet, and medicated washes from chemists, put up for acne, often helps, though like teenagers, the dogs often grow out of this condition. A Crested I bought-in had this condition in a bad way, but after a few weeks in the middle of my bed (yes, Cresteds always have their half of your bed in the middle!) and languishing among the best cushions, plus a twice weekly warm bath, soon had the skin as smooth as a babies rear.

A good diet does help and Cresteds will often sell their soul for a piece of fruit. Mine adore fresh greens which are chopped and added to grated carrot with their meals, and they also love curry.

Some breeders advocate strong medications, but my vet is anti-these and as Cresteds will lick anything you put on them (like cats) better to be safe than sorry. It is frightening to see some of the old recipes and remedies put into some of the old dog books.

I'm not against herbal products and many shampoos made from herbs can be beneficial. Herbal tea is much loved by Cresteds too. For the first time in years I have a good herb garden going, perhaps it has something to do with the fabulous Lincolnshire soil. I daily put a few handfuls of fresh parsley and other herbs, such as mint, thyme, savory and sorrel, into my 'Robot Chef' and mix it with the dogs scalded 'Winalot' meal and meat. I have to admit, my dogs are looking really well in spite of our wet weather. Years ago I fed fresh cow and sheep paunches to my Basenjis, Terriers and Toydogs, and they never looked better. My vet said green tripes were full of herbs and a dogs natural food. In recent years, I admit I have spent far more money on tinned and fresh butcher's meat and I never feel the dogs have the 'bloom' they used to have, and at far less cost. I do think the family hated the smell of the tripes and I hardly miss the trips to the slaughter house. In fact I have fed so many animals to my dogs over the years, I am almost a vegetarian.

But back to show preparation — good food, good husbandry and commonsense. A dog must be happy in himself to look good too. A sterile kennel may be OK but nothing makes a dog so happy as company of another dog or pet and human companionship. I know many invalids have toy dogs. They may not be able to give them walks and runs in the park, but if he has plenty of your love and a small garden to run in, plus the freedom of the house, you will be able to keep him in reasonable condition.

One of the first things you must do when you have entered for a show is to check that his nails are not too long. If you dare not cut them yourself ask your vet. It is always easier to trim nails after a bath, and after years of buying expensive nail clippers, I find that a good pair of scissors do the job cleanly and quickly. Just take a little off, at an angle, a little more off the top of the nail than underneath — see diagram.

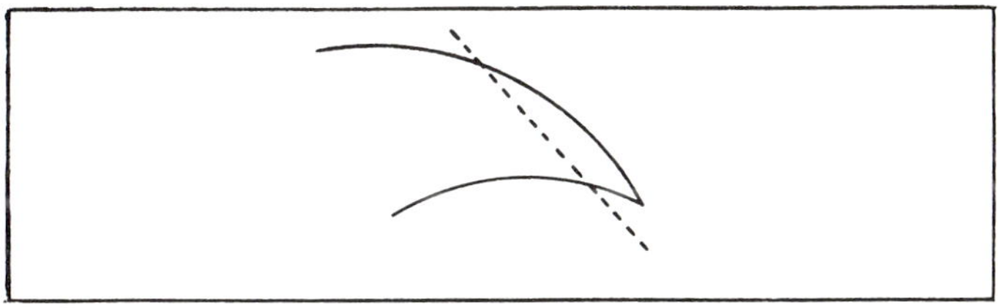

The quick will gradually creep back and provided he is walked on a hard surface part of the time his nails ought not to cause much trouble. A wood file too is a good idea: sit him comfortably on your lap and file down from the top, one way only and gently. If this is done twice a week it works as good as cutting. If you should cut the vein in the nail it may bleed like mad. However, don't panic, but have a few grains of Permanganate of Potash handy, put a good pinch on a dry sterile pad and press the nail into it. Your dog will probably end up with a purple nail but it will soon wear off.

A Crested has a hare foot which means long toes. He uses his toes to grip almost like fingers and the tightness and condition of his feet is mainly governed by exercise. A judge can see at once if the nails have been cut just before the show or if the dog is in naturally good muscle and body condition.

Your dog is now clean and ready and you should have a suitable box to take him to the show in. Many Cresteds suffer from car/travel-sickness so do not feed him before the show. There are travel pills on the market but these tend to dope toy dogs. You want yours to be bright and alert, so give him a full teaspoon of dry glucose, dropping it on his tongue. This has worked on my toy dogs over the years—especially with Basenjis, who are very prone to car sickness in the early years. Putting your dog in a box confines him, so make sure he has a thick clean towel to sit on. Most Cresteds seem to dribble rather than be actually sick. 'Jezabelle', one of my bitches, seems to loose a tremendous amount of fluid on any journey of more than five miles, and often looks terribly dehydrated when we arrive at the venue. She is gradually getting better and since having the glucose does not 'bring up her day' before dinner as she did. In fact I now feed just fresh raw meat (which is more digestible than meat cooked the night before) and this seems to help. If your dog is sick in a car and is not boxed, it tends to leap about and one rarely gets the smell out of the car for months. It goes behind the upholstery and as I tend to take my husband's car, I can be in the 'doghouse' for weeks. Don't forget to take your baby or medi wipes along!.

Crested hairless are really one of the easiest breeds to get ready for a show so take heart and show your puppy.

POWDER PUFFS

Because I think Powder Puffs ought to have separate classes in the show ring, I do not love them any-theless. But to me the Chinese Crested is the dainty hairless little dog, tossing his crest and having a look that no other little dog has. He is unique. The various types and coats of the Powder Puff, tells us about their ancestors. To me it is difficult to say there can be a set standard for them. I think they have a charm all their own and should be judged on soundness, temperament and to be as near to typical, in make and shape as their hairless siblings. They are true survivors — in a new-born litter they are the ones determined to live, never looking back from the day they are born. Often we have hand-fed the odd Powder Puff, hoping to give his hairless sibling more of a chance if the dam seemed not to be producing milk. On reflection, I suspect I was wrong, since it is better to keep the tough puppies sucking — the best chance of establishing a milk bar.

The Powder Puffs have everything to recommend them as super pets. They are if anything more biddable than the hairless brother. Almost without exception one could feel they were ideal candidates for natural obedience. Maybe having more hair, they have not such an acute sense of smell as have the hairless? This is a personal theory based upon observations of the breed these past twelve of more years.

They are usually fluffy in the nest, so look divine at six weeks. The coat tends to get more silky or of harder texture as he grows up. Most of the larger ones have the harsher coat, although as I have previously said, one can get a variant type of coat from the same sire and dam in the same and different litters.

So for show preparation it is just a question of having a healthy well-conditioned and well groomed dog. A bath before the show helps but the moment a judge puts his hands on your dog he can tell if the dog is light and shelly or firm and good to the touch.

It seems a fashion to clip the Powder Puff faces, making many of them look like little Afghans. Some of them look pretty and maybe it prevents beard staining, but it seems it is a matter of personal choice. I rather like the soft woolly look of the natural Powder Puff — although some have the shorter coat and do not grow fringes on the face.

Most of the Powder Puffs have good teeth and when bred to Hairless dogs produce often better mouths than many of the Hairless-to-Hairless offspring.

Some exhibitors tend to part their Powder Puffs coats but I note in the American Show scene it is thought preferable to show the dog in its natural state without clipping or hair partings.

Having been the poor relation of their Hairless brothers, the Powder Puff has indeed come to the fore, winning top honours in the ring, although we have yet to have a champion Powder Puff in the UK. They really are sweet little dogs and highly recommended as pets, perhaps standing up to the rough and tumble of young children better than the hairless ones.

Showing your dog can be a very enjoyable experience, but can be spoilt if you do not organise yourself properly. Here are a few tips:

Firstly, check all the details on the schedule carefully, then get the entries in to the Dog Secretary in good time and make a note of all the dates in your dog diary.

Obviously, you need to have your dog(s) as ready as possible for the great day. Take safe collars and leads, as well as your show leads. If you have bought swish show leads, get your dogs used to them before the event.

Take your dog(s) in show travel boxes if at all possible. Remember, you can travel with your dog on British Rail (the dog goes free) if the box is no more than 17" long. A box is useful, as this allows you in Train, Hotel and Motorway Buffets. Take a bag containing the dog dish and a bottle of glucose-laced milk to give on arrival — as this puts back some of the liquid he may have lost on the journey. A tasty snack, fresh meat, chicken or special tit-bit is usually appreciated.

You need a suitable rug for his pen and possibly go to town with matching draught-proof curtains. Take rubber boots if an outdoor show.

Make sure you have your entry pass and car pass if needed. It is often possible to pay for your catalogue with the entry fees, which is so useful and saves time. Always plan to get to the show in good time, as you need to get yourself and your dog ready for the fun and games of dog showing.

Some exhibitors like to take a snack for the dog in the ring. There is much mixed feelings about this, the important thing is not to disturb a fellow exhibitor and his/her exhibit. Do take a warm and waterproof jacket for yourself and a jacket for the dog. Our weather is variable to say the least. Have loose change handy. You may wish to ring home about that 1st prize, or decide to treat yourself to a drink to ease your disappointment.

Above all, show your good breeding and be generous in your congratulations to the winners. Your turn will come. I have shown my pets more time than I care to remember and believe that I will give up showing if I ever came home feeling cynical. It is now an expensive hobby, but to me and to many it is a form of escapism from domestic chores (remember I brought up five sons). On the whole it has enriched our lives, meeting many lovely folk and gaining many friends. The quick smart-Alecs of this world never seem to last for long. But the real dog enthusiast goes on for ever.....

Remember to order your doggy journal from your newsagent and this will inform and keep you in touch with all aspects of 'dogism'. If you take up showing remember it is meant to be a form of entertainment — it is not the be-all and end-all, and if you are out to make money, forget about dogs. Those dogs reputedly sold for thousands of pounds are few and far between. Not many part with a Crufts Supreme Best-In-Show Winner. In my varied life, where I have multiple hobbies, the Chinese Crested has been my most expensive so far, yet possibly one of my most enjoyable interests.

I hope he will never be commercialised and to me my CHINESE CRESTED DOG IS MY PRE-HISTORIC PET!

 Champion Handerby Snow Queen of Mesdames Andrews and Cardew.

& cc'c at Crufts

Do get a licence from the Post Office, when your Crested is six months old.

Do provide him with an interesting safe bone if you have to leave him, whilst in early puppyhood.

Do praise him when he makes a real effort to please you.

Do scold him if he is really naughty (tone of voice — far more effective than smacks).

Do be sensible about feeding time, a dog is a creature of habit.

Do teach him to spend a little time on his own —right from the start.

Do remember he is one of the cleverest dogs on earth. *You cannot brainwash him, but you can negotiate with him.*

Do ensure he can have a little free exercise each day, if only in the garden.

Do remember if you go to a dog show — it is meant to be enjoyed.

Do be a good sport and good manners never go unnoticed.

Do not leave him alone for hours. Chinese Cresteds love company, even if it is only the family cat.

Do make sure that your garden and gate is safe, a Crested is a born 'Houdini' and can get out of anywhere, should his mood move him, especially if a nearby bitch is in season.

Do examine his skin daily, any minor surface scratches will respond to a medicated cream.

Do keep chemical aerosols, bleach and weed killers away and never use slug pellets.

Do not use harsh substances on his skin or coat and remember that Cresteds wash like a cat.

Do not let him leap up at all and everyone. Some of your friends may treasure their nylons and clothes.

Do not let him foul footpaths but encourage him to use the hedgerow or gutter.

Do not encourage him to be naughty with other dogs, a dog in your arms usually tends to guard.

Do not over-feed your puppy late at night and not expect accidents on the floor.

Do not give old clothes, socks or shoes to chew, it is difficult for him to know the difference between your garden shoes and your best ones.

Do not push the responsibility of your pet on to others. He is yours and if you really love him, he will be yours always.

Do love your Crested at all times.

Mrs Foster Parker's Heathermount Voila (left) and Xotic (right)

Ought I to insure my Chinese Crested Dog?
Yes, you are legally responsible for any accident your dog may cause. It is possible to insure your dog through your household insurance policy for third party. However I recommend you take out a full comprehensive policy, to cover third party, death by accident, illness or disease, loss by stealing and straying, veterinary fees or loss of value. A Crested is an expensive and valued pet. Additional insurances can cover animals sent overseas and bitches in whelp. Many breeders give a preliminary insurance with each puppy sold. I suggest the new owner keeps this up. Better safe than sorry.

My puppy is car sick, what do I do?
Do not feed before the journey, feed raw meat the night before (easily digested). Give a full teaspoon full of dry glucose in a little water or directly onto the tongue.

Do you recommend my taking the dog in the car?
Chinese Cresteds on the whole love being in the car with you. Do if possible have a guard or use a travel box and never allow your pet on the front seat. Accidents can happen. Remember never to leave him in the car on a warm day, it becomes an oven.

If my puppy chews when I leave him alone, what do I do?
Make sure he has been properly exercised and fed before you go out. Provide him with a comfortable bed and a good safe bone. Do not leave any dog alone for long, he will only become frustrated and unhappy.

Will my Chinese Crested pine in kennels?
More than likely, ask the kennel owner to find a small friendly dog for him to share a kennel with. Two dogs are far easier to leave than one.

What do I do if my bitch gets accidentally mated?
Take veterinary advice at once.

Do I need to bath him often?
Not really, but Cresteds seem to adore baths. The Hairless dry almost at once, but Powder Puffs need to be thoroughly combed before a bath, otherwise dead hair in his coat will only tangle. Make sure you use the correct shampoo and dry with warm towels. If possible wash the Powder Puff on a sunny day so you can comb and brush him dry in the sunshine — far better than a dryer that may harm his coat.

My Crested has a violent tummy upset, what do I do?
If he is otherwise fit and well, rest his tummy and give him the white of one raw egg. If in doubt consult your vet — remember the dreaded Parvo starts with sickness.

May I change the brand of food occasionally?
Yes! Cresteds love variety the same as we do. Remember the top brands have had years of expense and research put into them.

Is it safe to use weed killers in the garden?
My vet says NO. Many weed killers are dangerous to dogs. One in particular has no known antidote.

My Crested is rather fat, what do I do?
Feed in the mornings only, some dogs seem to get fat through sheer contentment.

Does my Crested need to wear a coat?
No, nature compensates and most Hairless have a normal temperature of 103°; the Powder Puffs seem to be the normal 101.4^{o}. However, many exhibitors find show benches rather cold and your dog may feel more secure 'rugged' up in a warm jacket. Do remember many Hairless are allergic to wool, so line his coat with silk or cotton. Many US Cresteds I am told, boast magnificent wardrobes.

How often do I worm my Crested?
Regularly; your vet will supply the latest and most sophisticated drugs for worms.

Can anyone go to a dog show?
Yes, for a small entrance fee. You will always find someone to chat to, and no one need ever feel lonely whilst dog shows exist.

Do you think one should keep ones pet alive as long as possible?
No, quality of life is all that matters. If your pet no longer enjoys life and is suffering, it is far kinder to have your vet put him to sleep.

Is it very upsetting?
No, with modern drugs (remember the animals get them before we do) your pet will not feel a thing. You will naturally be upset, a pet is part of ones family, and often ones best friend, but your beloved dogs feelings should come before yours.

Is it a good idea to get another dog at once?
This is up to you, remember no two dogs are alike. Do not expect a successor to be a replica of the other. A new puppy is going to be far more active than an old dog.

Need I buy the most expensive dog food?
No, shop around, but as with our own food we pay for expensive packaging. Fresh meat and offal is far cheaper than tinned food.

We are at work all day, is it fair to keep a Chinese Crested?
No, this breed needs companionship. A Crested on its own for hours may become miserable and bark and howl. If a dog is left for a few hours, he should at least have another pet to keep him company. An old Basenji my father-in-law had (yes Basenjis and Cresteds) are identical in character) would only be happy if the pet tortoise shared her basket. Another of our Basenjis would stay happily alone if the old Macaw was in the room. Having a dog of any breed is like having a child in the house. Only have a Chinese Crested if you wish to belong to him for the rest of his days.

The information covering the Xoloitzcuintli and Moonflower Dogs on the following page has been kindly supplied by the Dutch authority on hairless dogs, Mr Hugo Hernandez.

THE XOLOITZCUINTLI:
First Dog of the Americas

The Xoloitzcuintli (pronounced show-low-eats-queen-tlee) or Standard Mexican Hairless is one of the world's oldest and rarest dogs. It is believed to be the first distinct breed of canine to make its appearance in the Americas having accompanied the earliest migrations of man across the Bering Straits.

Clay figures representing this animal have been found which date as early as 1500 BC. From the Colima culture of Western Mexico, dating from 300 to 900 AD archaeologists have collected over five hundred ceramic effigies of the 'Standard Mexican Hairless' while probing ancient burial sites. These dogs or their clay representations were buried with the dead in the belief that they guided the souls of the departed to their final resting place while also providing sustenance along the way.

The history of the Xoloitzcuintli (Xolo for short) among the Aztecs is well documented not only in the Indian codices, but in the accounts of the Spanish chroniclers who accompanied the Conquistadores. They reported seeing caged or tethered hairless dogs being sold in the market place of Tenochtitlan, the Aztec capital. The Aztecs bred these animals selectively, prizing them as house pets, bedwarmers and sacrificial offerings. They also fattened them for the table, considering them great culinary delicacies — a taste which they passed on to their Spanish conquerors.

Since the Xoloitzcuintli was slaughtered indiscriminately in post-conquest days while no effort was made to perpetuate his kind, he became nearly extinct, surviving only in the more remote villages. It was not until the mid-1950s that an organised effort was launched under the auspices of the ACM (Mexican Kennel Club) to rescue and re-establish the breed. Currently there are about a hundred registered examples and perhaps several hundred unregistered individuals which may be roaming the hinterlands or have somehow made their way into the hands of American tourists.

Among the present day country folk of Mexico the Xolo has the reputation, persisting since pre-Columbian times, of warding off or curing numerous ailments from the common cold to rheumatism. The older generation still take these dogs to bed with them. No doubt their canine warmth, remarkably feverish with no hair to insulate it, actually does have palliative powers.

The modern Xolo need not rely on magic to achieve status in today's canine world, however. He has been immortalised by Mexico's late great Diego Rivera, appearing in some of his best known murals (one of which is on view in the Hotel del Prado lobby, Mexico City), and he also figures importantly in the recent Chapultepec Castle murals of renowned artist-architect Juan O'Gorman.

In addition, he has won the admiration and approval of dog fanciers all over the world. *Quetzalcoatl*, presently considered one of the top Xolo studs in Mexico, was campaigned widely in Europe during the Spring of 1967 by his owner, the Countess Lascelles de Premio Real, and became the very first Mexican dog ever to win a *bonafide* International Championship. Now he has many sons and daughters who also bear the title of 'Champion'.

In the show ring or out, Xolos always manage to draw and captivate a crowd. People are not only amazed to see a truly hairless dog, but are startled to note the statuesque proportions and sleek aristocratic bearing of this animal that they had always imagined as Chihuahua-like. Indeed the Xoloitzcuintli, looking somewhat like an under-sized Doberman, is no toy! He measures around twenty inches at the withers and while he's small enough to invite on the sofa, he's large enough to discourage intruders.

In short, the Xoloitzcuintli is almost ideally suited to being a friend to man. He not only offers exotic beauty, grace and elegance together with intelligence and good temperament, but he qualifies as the perfect house pet since his hairlessness makes him clean, flealess, odourless and hypoallerenic.

HISTORY OF THE PERUVIAN INCA ORCHID MOONFLOWER DOGS

This very gentle breed is an ancient one from Peru. The Peruvian Indians are a most gentle people, hence, these dogs have no memory pattern of harsh treatment and are easily intimidated when placed in a gruff atmosphere. These dogs of Peru respond only to kind and gentle treatment, and respond with fierce devotion. Rough deportment, whether physical or vocal only produces spiritlessness or rebellion.

The Indians of the Latin American countries are of Asiatic descent. They believe they orginated in China, and the dogs accompanied them on their migration to these continents.

Quechua is the language of the Peruvian Indian. In this tongue the dog is called Caa-Allepo, which means 'Dog without Vestments'.

When Pizzarro and his men came to Peru, they discovered the Incas had a messenger and delivery service. From the sea coast back into the oriente or Amazon area they had established stations every eight miles, the distance a man could run at full speed. A runner could start out from either end and carry messages and a small pack to jungle chieftains or highly prized Orchids to coastal rulers. The Orchids would be used to decorate the cool dark rooms of the homes of the powerful, wherein, by day, the light skinned dogs would be kept from the damaging rays of the sun. This is what the Conquistadores saw upon their arrival: these strangely beautiful dogs among the Orchid blooms. Hence the name, Perros Flora, or 'Flower Dogs' — and the flower was always an Orchid.

The Moon Dogs, because of their very light colouring, due to a lack of melanin, were kept inside during the day because the sun's hot rays could be disastrous to their sensitive skin and only allowed to run by the light of the moon. The nobility decreed that the village dogs, most of whom were solid black, brown, red, grey and the Powder Puff variety must be kept locked up while their dogs ran. They kept some Powder Puffs, but only the best. Thus they lessened the risk of misalliances between the commoner's dog and a noble dog. The nobility coveted light dogs, and vied with one another to acquire the lightest hued dogs possible, or the best marked puff variety. The villagers also sought to breed good dogs to exchange for favours from the nobility.

The Inca Nobles were noted for selective breeding among themselves often brother and sister marriages. Purity and predictability was their aim and they carried it into their canine development.

Today the Indians of Peru, the pure descendants of the Incas keep and breed these dogs.

KENNEL CLUB BREED STANDARD OF THE CHINESE CRESTED DOG

GENERAL APPEARANCE — A small, active and graceful dog; medium to fine boned, smooth hairless body, with hair on feet, head and tail only or covered with a soft veil of hair.

CHARACTERISTICS — Two distinct types of breed: Deer type, racy and fine boned, and Cobby type — heavier in body and bone.

TEMPERAMENT — Happy, never vicious.

HEAD & SKULL — Slightly rounded and elongated skull. Cheeks cleanly chiselled, lean and flat, tapering into muzzle. Stop slightly pronounced but not extreme. Head smooth, without excess wrinkles. Distance from base of skull to stop equal to distance from stop to tip of nose. Muzzle tapering slightly but never pointed, lean without flews. Nose a prominent feature, narrow in keeping with muzzle. Any colour nose acceptable. Head presenting graceful appearance, with alert expression and no suggestion of coarseness or raciness. Lips tight and thin; ideally, crest beginning at the top of head tapering off down neck. Head itself may flow to any length, a long and flowing crest preferred, but sparse acceptable.

EYES — So dark as to appear black. Little or no white showing. Medium size. Set wide apart.

EARS — Set low: highest point of base of ear level with outside corner of eye. Large and erect, with or without fringe, except in Powder Puffs where drop ears are permissible.

MOUTH — Jaws strong, with perfect, regular scissor bite i.e. the upper teeth closely overlapping the lower teeth and set square to the jaws.

NECK — Lean, free from throatiness, long and sloping gracefully into strong shoulders. When moving, carried high and slightly arched.

FOREQUARTERS — Shoulders clean, narrow and well laid back. Legs long and slender, set well under body. Elbows held close to body. Pasterns fine, strong, nearly vertical. Toes turned neither in nor out.

BODY — Medium to long. Supple. Chest broad and deep, not barrel-ribbed. Breast bone not prominent. Brisket extending to elbows; moderate tuck-up.

HINDQUARTERS — Rump well-rounded and muscular, loins taut, stifles firm and long, sweeping into the well let-down hock. Angulation of the rear limb must be such as to produce a level back. Hind-legs set wide apart.

FEET — Extreme hare foot, narrow and very long, with unique elongation of small bones between joints, especially in forefeet, which almost appear to possess an extra joint. Nails any colour, moderately long. Socks ideally confined to toes, but not extending above top of pastern. Feet turning neither in nor out.

TAIL — Set high, carried up or out when in motion. Long and tapering, fairly straight, not curled or twisted to either side, falling naturally when at rest. Plume long and flowing, confined to lower two-thirds or tail. Sparse plume acceptable.

MOVEMENT — Long, flowing and elegant with good reach and plenty of drive.

COAT — No large patches of hair anywhere on body. Skin fine grained, smooth, warm to the touch. In Powder Puffs coat consists of an undercoat with soft veil of long hair, veil coat a feature.

COLOUR — Any colour or combination of colours.

SIZE — Ideal height in dogs: 28 - 33cm (11" - 13") at withers. Bitches: 23 - 30cm (9" - 12") at withers. Weight varies considerably, but should not be over 5½ kgs (12lbs).

FAULTS — Any departure from the foregoing points should be considered a fault and the seriousness of the fault should be in exact proportion to its degree.

NOTE — Male animals should have two apparently normal testicles fully descended into the scrotum.

AMERICAN KENNEL CLUB STANDARD FOR CHINESE CRESTED (HAIRLESS)

GENERAL APPEARANCE — Slender, fine-boned, active and graceful. The body smooth and hairless except for hair on head, lower legs, feet and plume on tail.

HEAD — Slightly rounded skull. Distance to slight stop equal to distance from stop to tip of nose. Cheeks taper cleanly into muzzle.

EARS — Large and erect placed so that the base of the ear is level with the outside corner of the eye.

EYES — Dark, almond-shaped and set wide apart.

NOSE — Level or scissors bite, with pre-molars absent. (With hairless factor, teeth other than pre-molars are frequently missing).

NECK AND BODY — Neck is lean and clean, slightly arched from the withers to the base of the skull, carried high. Brisket extends to elbow, breast-bone not overly prominent. Chest deep, tapering to a moderate tuckup at the flanks. Length of body slightly longer than height at withers. Topline level.

TAIL — Long, straight and tapering - carried gaily or straight out when in motion. Two-thirds of the end of the tail is covered by a long, flowing plume.

FOREQUARTERS — Shoulders clean and narrow, angulated to allow good reach. Elbows well knit. Pasterns fine and strong. Legs long, slender and straight.

FEET — Same as forequarters.

COAT — Head Crest begins at the stop and tapers off between the base of skull and back of neck. Texture is soft and silky, flowing to any length. Socks on feet are ideally confined to toes, but should not extend above pastern or hock joint.

COLOR — Any color or combination of colors.

GAIT — Smooth and flowing.

SIZE — Males not to exceed 13 inches at the withers; females not to exceed 12 inches at the withers.

TEMPERAMENT — Gay and alert.

AMERICAN KENNEL CLUB STANDARD FOR CHINESE CRESTED (POWDER PUFF)

The Powder Puff is judged by the same standard as the Hairless except:

COAT — Undercoat of hair all over is very short; guard hairs are thin and longer, creating a veil-like effect. Texture is soft and silky.

TEETH — Level or scissors bite with full dentition.

A Victorian Chinese Crested Dog, Chinese Emperor.

USEFUL INFORMATION

First Breed Classes were at Brent, London 1971.

First Chinese Crested Dog Club show, 28 September 1974.

First arrival of foundation stock of our present day Cresteds in 1965 - Mrs Harris's *Alta of Cresthaven.* The main bloodlines are *Cresthaven-Lee* lines.

The first championship Chinese Crested Dog Show Saturday 3 August 1985; Judge Mrs Mary Smith *(Clogheen).*

First Challenge Certificates awarded to the breed Crufts 1982, C.C. Dog: Mrs Harbottle's *Aes to Dynasty;* reserve C.C. Mr & Mrs Jones' *Jasper of Kojak.* Bitches: C.C. Mr & Mrs Jones' *Krystal of Kojak*; reserve C.C. *Pekevista Mei Mei Shan of Aes.*

First UK Champion (dog): *Champion Aes to Dynasty.*

First UK Champion (bitch): *Champion Krystal of Kojak.*

First Irish Champion: *Champion Staround Jacko (first of breed in Europe).*

First Australian Champion and Chinese Crested Dog to win Supreme Best in Show all breeds at a Major Australian Metropolitan Championship show in a huge entry, Mrs Wendye Slayter and Peter Warby's *Aus Champion St Erme Crested Pony*, under famous Australian judge, Mr Bob L'Opesto.

CLUB DETAILS

THE CHINESE CRESTED DOG CLUB

This, the only official Club in the UK was founded in 1969. Its foundation officers were: Mrs R. Harris (Chairman), the late Mrs J. Forster (Secretary), Mrs D. Tyler (Treasurer); *Committee:* Mesdames Crowther-Davies, Mooney, Jennings, Land and Enders, Misses Pontin and Fairs and Mr Smith.

Present day Club officials include: Mrs D. Crowther-Davies (President), W. F. Parker Esq (Chairman), A. T. Broadhead Esq (Secretary). Enquires to Mr Broadhead, 83 Gorge Road, Coseley, Bilston, Wolverhampton, Staffs, UK.

THE KENNEL CLUB: 1 Clarges Street, Piccadily, London W1Y 8AB.

THE AMERICAN CHINESE CRESTED CLUB

President & Secretary: Mr Dick Dickerson, Box 2025, 2706 Murfreesboro Road, Nashville, Tennessee 37214, USA; Registrar: Mrs Jo-Ann Orlik, RR 1, Box 27, Thompson Bridge Road, Jackson, New Jersey 08527, USA; Treasurer: Mrs Jean Scott, 6154 Mt View Road, Antioch, Tennessee 37013, USA.